PILLAR
BOX
RED

in association with

MATCH!
THE BEST FOOTBALL MAGAZINE!

ISBN: 978-1-914536-88-5

Photographs: © Getty Images

FOOTBALL SKILLS

2024

Written by
Jared Tinslay

Designed by
Darryl Tooth

CONTENTS

SKILLS ICON NO.1
JAY-JAY OKOCHA

The seven-time Nigerian Footballer of the Year spent his childhood playing footy on the streets of his hometown with anything that he could find that was round – and that shaped his style for the rest of his career! Every time he stepped onto the pitch, it was like he was reliving those days with his mates, playing with the freedom of youth. After spells in Germany and Turkey, he spent four years at PSG before balling at Bolton back when they were in the Premier League!

DID YOU KNOW? ONE OF THE PREM'S GREATEST-EVER SHOWMEN ALSO HAPPENS TO BE THE UNCLE OF PREMIER LEAGUE MIDFIELDER ALEX IWOBI!

TOP SKILL! THE SOMBRERO

CAREER LEAGUE STATS

Date	Club	Games	Goals
1990-1992	Borussia Neunkirchen	35	7
1992-1996	Eintracht Frankfurt	90	18
1996-1998	Fenerbahce	62	30
1998-2002	PSG	114	12
2002-2006	Bolton	124	14
2006-2007	Qatar SC	41	6
2007-2008	Hull	18	0

FACTPACK!
Full Name: Augustine Azuka Okocha
DOB: 14/08/1973
Height: 5ft 9in
Country: Algeria
Caps: 73
Goals: 14

SHOWREEL! Scan the QR

CONFIDENCE 95
DRIBBLING 96
TRICKS 99
AGILITY 95
WEAK FOOT 85

MATCH! 14 / MATCH! 15

SKILLS ICON NO.2
RONALDINHO

DID YOU KNOW? WHEN THE SAMBA STAR WAS SIGNED BY BARCELONA IN 2003, OVER 25,000 FANS WENT TO THE NOU CAMP TO SEE HIM PRESENTED AS THEIR PLAYER!

Loads of today's top tricksters refer to Ronaldinho as their football idol, he was so fun to watch! He grew up playing footy on the Brazilian beaches of Porto Alegre, before making a name for himself as a teenage prodigy by scoring all 23 goals in a 23-0 win for his junior side. After signing for PSG as a 21-year-old wonderkid, he briefly played with fellow footy skills legend Jay-Jay Okocha, but had his most successful spell at Barcelona – where he lifted the Champions League and Ballon d'Or!

TOP SKILL! THE ELASTICO

FACTPACK!
Full Name: Ronaldo de Assis Moreira
DOB: 21/03/1980
Height: 6ft 0in
Country: Brazil
Caps: 97
Goals: 33

SHOWREEL! Scan the QR code to watch some of his best bits!

CAREER LEAGUE STATS

Date	Club	Games	Goals
1998-2001	Gremio	89	47
2001-2003	PSG	55	17
2003-2008	Barcelona	145	70
2008-2011	Milan	76	20
2011-2012	Flamengo	56	23

CONFIDENCE 100
DRIBBLING 98
TRICKS 100
AGILITY 96
WEAK FOOT 88

MATCH! 22 / MATCH! 23

SKILLS ICON NO.3
MARADONA

CAREER LEAGUE STATS

Date	Club	Games	Goals
1976-1981			
1981-1982	Boca Juniors	40	28
1982-1984	Barcelona		
1984-1991	Napoli	188	81
1993-1994	Newell's Old Boys		
1995-1997			

Maradona received his first football as a present when he was just three years old and soon became obsessed with the game. He made his senior debut in Argentina when he was 15 and quickly attracted attention from Europe's biggest clubs. After a two-season spell with Barcelona, he moved to Napoli and became a legend, winning two Serie A titles there. His greatest moment came at the 1986 World Cup, however, where he captained his nation to the trophy and scored one of the tournament's best-ever individual goals against England. We just won't mention the Hand of God...

DID YOU KNOW? HE PLAYED ONE GAME IN A TOTTENHAM SHIRT – IT WAS A TESTIMONIAL FOR THEIR FORMER ARGENTINE PLAYER OSSIE ARDILES!

TOP SKILL! THE MARADONA TURN

FACTPACK!
Full name: Diego Armando Maradona
DOB: 30/10/1960
Height: 5ft 5in
Country: Argentina
Caps: 91
Goals: 34

SHOWREEL!

CONFIDENCE 100
DRIBBLING 99
TRICKS 100
AGILITY 97
WEAK FOOT 75

MATCH! 36 / MATCH! 37

SKILLS ICON NO.4
ZIDANE

CAREER LEAGUE STATS

TOP SKILL! THE ROULETTE

DID YOU KNOW? HIS TRANSFER TO REAL MADRID IN 2001 FROM JUVENTUS WAS A WORLD RECORD FEE AT THE TIME OF €77.5 MILLION!

CONFIDENCE 99
DRIBBLING 97
TRICKS 98
AGILITY 80
WEAK FOOT 97

ZINEDINE ZIDANE 56

CROSSWORD

WHO STARTED WHERE?

ODD ONE OUT!

COOL QUIZZES 20, 30, 44 & 58

COMPETITION

PICK YOUR TOP 5 FAVE SKILLERS!

MUDRYK Chelsea & Ukraine

DEPAY Atletico Madrid & Netherlands

DIAZ Liverpool & Colombia

JESUS Arsenal & Brazil

RODRYGO Real Madrid & Brazil

FODEN Man. City & England

WIN! RIG 300 PRO GAMING HEADSET!

COMPETITION 54

50

ALEJANDRO GARNACHO

Club: Man. United
Country: Argentina
DOB: 01/07/2004

In last year's Skills Annual, we had Amad Diallo in 50th spot on our countdown, but this year he's been replaced by another United wonderkid! That's not to say Diallo is too far behind – he had a sick season on loan at Sunderland in 2022-23 and caught our eye in the EFL along with the likes of Joao Pedro and Iliman Ndiaye! But Garnacho's worthy of making our Top 50 list this year – his potential is absolutely limitless!

CONFIDENCE	DRIBBLING	TRICKS	AGILITY	WEAK FOOT
79	79	76	86	79

49

OLEKSANDR ZINCHENKO

Club: Arsenal
Country: Ukraine
DOB: 15/12/1996

Have you seen the video of Zinchenko participating in Puma's Control Challenge? If not, drop what you're doing and search for it! He had MATCH drooling with his third effort, which was quite simply silly, but we weren't too surprised – Kyle Walker once said that "Zinny" was the most technical player in the Man. City squad!

CONFIDENCE	DRIBBLING	TRICKS	AGILITY	WEAK FOOT
88	80	76	80	75

48

ALEXANDER ISAK

⭐ TOP SKILL!
THE BALL ROLL

Club: Newcastle
Country: Sweden
DOB: 21/09/1999

In 2016, the silky Sweden striker was compared to international legend Zlatan Ibrahimovic – famous for his arrogance, agility and acrobatic flicks! Isak definitely has a bit of Zlatan about him, but it's his top technique and touch – just check out his mad dribbling assist v Everton last season – rather than his larger-than-life personality that grabs the attention!

CONFIDENCE	DRIBBLING	TRICKS	AGILITY	WEAK FOOT
80	80	75	77	88

47

WILLIAN

Club: *Fulham*
Country: *Brazil*
DOB: *09/08/1988*

When you look through the history books you'll read about different periods of planet Earth, like the Prehistoric Period, the Middle Ages or the Renaissance Era. Well, right now we're living in the Willian Renaissance! Fulham fans will be overjoyed that the veteran winger has rediscovered his epic Chelsea form rather than his Arsenal one!

TOP SKILL!
THE DRAG BACK

CONFIDENCE	DRIBBLING	TRICKS	AGILITY	WEAK FOOT
82	81	80	82	78

46

XAVI SIMONS

Club: *RB Leipzig*
Country: *Netherlands*
DOB: *21/04/2003*

One of MATCH's favourite hobbies is scouting outside of Europe's top five leagues for the next big talent – and ex-Barcelona youth prospect Simons is just that! We think French giants PSG made the right choice in re-signing him last summer, before sending him on loan to RB Leipzig, because he showed just how good he can be at PSV in 2022-23!

CONFIDENCE	DRIBBLING	TRICKS	AGILITY	WEAK FOOT
80	85	82	90	75

45

PHIL FODEN

Club: *Man. City*
Country: *England*
DOB: *28/05/2000*

MATCH is going to get in touch with NASA to see if they can send a football on one of their rockets into space and then let it drop, because we think the City academy ace would still be able to control it - even if it came hurtling at the speed of light, covered in icy stalactites!

CONFIDENCE	DRIBBLING	TRICKS	AGILITY	WEAK FOOT
85	86	80	90	75

44

BUKAYO SAKA

Club: Arsenal
Country: England
DOB: 05/09/2001

Arsenal fans chant that Saka's dynamite - and he has certainly "exploded" over the last two years! He's recorded more than 40 Premier League goals and assists combined since the start of the 2021-22 season - more than any other Gunner - adding end product to his mazy dribbles!

CONFIDENCE	DRIBBLING	TRICKS	AGILITY	WEAK FOOT
90	90	78	88	72

43

ENDRICK

Club: Palmeiras
Country: Brazil
DOB: 21/07/2006

Forget worrying about GCSE results and potential prom dates, Endrick was getting signed by Real Madrid when he was 16 years old! The giants agreed to pay Palmeiras €70 million for the mega exciting wonderkid, although he can't join them officially until he turns 18 in July 2024. He'll shoot up this list once he proves himself at Los Blancos!

CONFIDENCE	DRIBBLING	TRICKS	AGILITY	WEAK FOOT
85	88	88	85	73

42

WILFRIED GNONTO

Club: Leeds
Country: Italy
DOB: 05/11/2003

The Italian pocket rocket isn't far off from being the shortest player in world footy, but the saying goes that good things come in small packages - and Gnonto is living proof! As well as having a killer first touch, his low centre of gravity means he can wriggle his way past his opponents with ease!

CONFIDENCE	DRIBBLING	TRICKS	AGILITY	WEAK FOOT
80	85	86	90	78

41

EBERECHI EZE

Club: Crystal Palace
Country: England
DOB: 29/06/1998

MATCH is gonna buy Eze a pair of rollerskates for Xmas this year, because he could become a pro skater the way he glides across the football pitch! Or maybe the baller is destined to appear on celebrity Dancing On Ice once he eventually retires from football!

CONFIDENCE	DRIBBLING	TRICKS	AGILITY	WEAK FOOT
86	86	85	86	80

40

CRISTIANO RONALDO

CONFIDENCE 95

DRIBBLING 82

TRICKS 85

AGILITY 74

WEAK FOOT 88

Club: *Al Nassr*

Country: *Portugal*

DOB: *05/02/1985*

Whatever you think about the way Ronaldo left Man. United to join the Saudi league, you can't deny the man his legendary status! In fact, CR7 has achieved so much in football we reckon he should become UNESCO World Heritage or otherwise one of the wonders of the modern world. LOL!

MATCH!
WOMEN SKILLERS

DEBINHA

FACTFILE!

DOB: 20/10/1991
Position: Forward
Club: Kansas City Current
Country: Brazil
Boot brand: Nike

DID YOU KNOW?

Her football idol growing up was none other than Brazil legend Ronaldinho!

FACTFILE!

DOB: 04/02/1994
Position: Att. midfielder
Club: Barcelona
Country: Spain
Boot brand: Nike

DID YOU KNOW?
She's the first player to win UEFA Women's Player of the Year and Ballon d'Or Femenin twice in a row!

PUTELLAS

JAY-JAY OKOCHA

The seven-time Nigerian Footballer of the Year spent his childhood playing footy on the streets of his hometown with anything that he could find that was round – and that shaped his style for the rest of his career! Every time he stepped onto the pitch, it was like he was reliving those days with his mates, playing with the freedom of youth. After spells in Germany and Turkey, he spent four years at PSG before balling at Bolton back when they were in the Premier League!

FACTPACK!

Full Name: *Augustine Azuka Okocha*

DOB: 14/08/1973

Height: 5ft 9in

Country: Nigeria

Caps: 73

Goals: 14

CAREER LEAGUE STATS

Date	Club	Games	Goals
1990-1992	Borussia Neunkirchen	35	7
1992-1996	Eintracht Frankfurt	90	18
1996-1998	Fenerbahce	62	30
1998-2002	PSG	84	12
2002-2006	Bolton	124	14
2006-2007	Qatar SC	41	6
2007-2008	Hull	18	0

TOP SKILL!

THE SOMBRERO

DID YOU KNOW?

ONE OF THE PREM'S GREATEST-EVER SHOWMEN ALSO HAPPENS TO BE THE UNCLE OF PREMIER LEAGUE MIDFIELDER ALEX IWOBI!

CONFIDENCE
95

DRIBBLING
96

TRICKS
99

AGILITY
95

WEAK FOOT
85

SHOWREEL!

Scan the QR code to watch some of his best bits!

39

HAKIM ZIYECH

CONFIDENCE
80

DRIBBLING
83

TRICKS
92

AGILITY
85

WEAK FOOT
72

Club: Galatasaray
Country: Morocco
DOB: 19/03/1993

Poor Ziyech has gone from 9th, to 19th to 39th in the space of three years! He started just six Premier League matches for Chelsea in 2022-23 to confirm his decline, but he's got enough skiller points in the bag to keep his name on the countdown. He needs to up his game at Gala to not get ousted next year, though!

38

AZZEDINE OUNAHI

Club: Marseille
Country: Morocco
DOB: 19/04/2000

When we think about Ounahi, MATCH instantly remembers the 2022 World Cup – and we can picture the Morocco marvel making Spain's insanely good midfield look pretty average! The way he plays with such swagger and style makes it seem as if he were playing on the streets!

CONFIDENCE	DRIBBLING	TRICKS	AGILITY	WEAK FOOT
88	88	88	82	78

37

PEDRI

Club: Barcelona
Country: Spain
DOB: 25/11/2002

We've got a great little nugget (of information, not chicken!) for you guys… When Pedri first joined his hometown's academy as a child, he was originally a centre-back! Thankfully for everyone involved, they realised he was far more useful further up the pitch, where he could dazzle defenders with his quick feet and vision!

CONFIDENCE	DRIBBLING	TRICKS	AGILITY	WEAK FOOT
85	87	80	90	85

36

JACK GREALISH

Club: Man. City
Country: England
DOB: 10/09/1995

We're pretty sure that when Grealish agreed to join sports brand Puma in 2023, they must have been working together on a new stealth boot… One that literally makes the ball glue to your feet when you dribble! How else can he keep it that close to his body otherwise?

TOP SKILL!
THE BODY FEINT

CONFIDENCE	DRIBBLING	TRICKS	AGILITY	WEAK FOOT
90	92	80	85	80

35

NABIL FEKIR

Club: *Real Betis*
Country: *France*
DOB: *18/07/1993*

One of the biggest tragedies in Premier League history is Fekir's failed transfer to Liverpool! He was literally on the verge of signing for The Reds in the summer of 2018, but an issue arose with his agent and the plug was well and truly pulled. We've been robbed of him in the PL!

CONFIDENCE	DRIBBLING	TRICKS	AGILITY	WEAK FOOT
94	88	84	81	80

34

MICHAEL OLISE

Club: *Crystal Palace*
Country: *France*
DOB: *12/12/2001*

The "Champs-Elysees" is one of the most elegant streets in the whole of Paris – the French capital known for its Fashion Week – while the "Michael-Olise" just happens to be one of the most elegant footballers in the Premier League. Plus he represents Les Bleus internationally!

CONFIDENCE	DRIBBLING	TRICKS	AGILITY	WEAK FOOT
86	89	84	92	76

33

PAUL POGBA

TOP SKILL!
THE PIROUETTE

Club: *Juventus*
Country: *France*
DOB: *15/03/1993*

Pogba has suffered something of a confidence crisis since re-joining Juventus, not helped by all his injuries. It's for that reason that the baller finds himself ten places lower than in last year's countdown, although we're hoping he'll rediscover his mojo before next year's one comes around!

CONFIDENCE	DRIBBLING	TRICKS	AGILITY	WEAK FOOT
82	88	92	77	88

TOP SKILL!
FAKE RIGHT AND GO

32

SAMUEL CHUKWUEZE

Club: AC Milan
Country: Nigeria
DOB: 22/05/1999

The Nigeria international revealed a few years ago that his big hero growing up was fellow countryman Jay-Jay Okocha – and we get those vibes when we see him play! He produces some jaw-dropping tekkers and the only reason the left-footed winger isn't further up this list is because he often only uses his right foot to stand on!

CONFIDENCE	DRIBBLING	TRICKS	AGILITY	WEAK FOOT
89	88	94	86	70

31

MEMPHIS DEPAY

Club: Atletico Madrid
Country: Netherlands
DOB: 13/02/1994

We know the former Barcelona flop is a rapper, so we thought we'd spit him some bars… "You've gone from 14th place to 31, you've lost some pace and you're not so young, you've still got skills although your ranking is worse, just stay away from that Camp Nou curse!" Well, we tried…

CONFIDENCE	DRIBBLING	TRICKS	AGILITY	WEAK FOOT
87	88	92	83	77

30

GABRIEL JESUS

Club: Arsenal
Country: Brazil
DOB: 03/04/1997

We've seen the twinkled-toed striker produce some crazy skills to hold up play and keep possession, as well as to create space in the box to get a shot off! We didn't miss his no-look pass against Liverpool last season either, which must have been a nod to Brazilian team-mate Roberto Firmino in the opposition colours!

CONFIDENCE	DRIBBLING	TRICKS	AGILITY	WEAK FOOT
89	87	86	91	74

WORDFIT

Fit the skillers that just missed out on this year's countdown into the giant grid!

Bellingham	Firmino	Neto
Boufal	Gnabry	Pellistri
Camavinga	Guimaraes	Pedro
Cherki	Havertz	Podence
Coutinho	Kulusevski	Sarr
Diallo	Martial	Sinisterra
Di Maria	Mbeumo	Sterling
Doku	Nani	Taarabt
Dybala	Ndiaye	Trossard
Fati	Neres	Wirtz

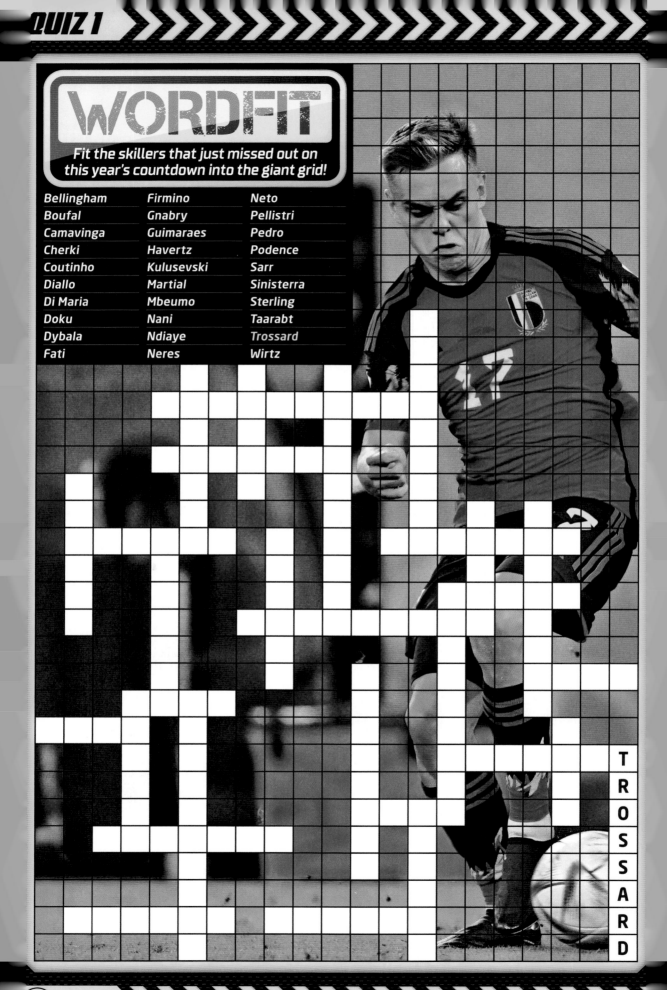

T
R
O
S
S
A
R
D

5 QUESTIONS ON...
DEBINHA

1 How old will the Brazil baller be come Christmas 2023 – 30, 32 or 34 years old?

2 Which shirt number does she wear for her club Kansas City Current – No.9, No.19 or No.99?

3 Which NWSL club was she playing for before joining Kansas City in 2023 – North Carolina Courage, Orlando Pride or OL Reign?

4 How many caps has she won for Brazil – more or less than 125?

5 True or False? She had a brief loan spell at Women's Super League side Chelsea back in 2012!

SPOT THE BALL!

Mark where you think the ball should be in this cool action shot!

ANSWER ON P6

RONALDINHO

Loads of today's top tricksters refer to Ronaldinho as their football idol, as he was so fun to watch! He grew up playing footy on the Brazilian beaches of Porto Alegre, before making a name for himself as a teenage prodigy by scoring all 23 goals in a 23-0 win for his junior side. After signing for PSG as a 21-year-old wonderkid, he briefly played with fellow footy skills legend Jay-Jay Okocha, but had his most successful spell at Barcelona – where he lifted the Champions League and Ballon d'Or!

FACTPACK!

Full name: *Ronaldo de Assis Moreira*

DOB: *21/03/1980*

Height: *6ft 0in*

Country: *Brazil*

Caps: *97*

Goals: *33*

CAREER LEAGUE STATS

Date	Club	Games	Goals
1998–2001	*Gremio*	89	47
2001–2003	*PSG*	55	17
2003–2008	*Barcelona*	145	70
2008–2011	*Milan*	76	20
2011–2012	*Flamengo*	56	23
2012–2014	*Atletico Mineiro*	58	20
2014–2015	*Queretaro*	25	8
2015	*Fluminense*	7	0

DID YOU KNOW?

WHEN THE SAMBA STAR WAS SIGNED BY BARCELONA IN 2003, OVER 25,000 FANS WENT TO THE NOU CAMP TO SEE HIM PRESENTED AS THEIR PLAYER!

TOP SKILL!
THE ELASTICO

SHOWREEL!

Scan the QR code to watch some of his best bits!

CONFIDENCE
100

DRIBBLING
98

TRICKS
100

AGILITY
96

WEAK FOOT
88

29

LUCAS PAQUETA

Club: West Ham
Country: Brazil
DOB: 27/08/1997

We all know that The Hammers are forever blowing bubbles, but Paqueta is so packed with tricks he wouldn't be blowing the ones that burst within seconds! Nah, he'd be there with the huge loop and wand, producing bubbles that become so big you could basically fit inside them!

CONFIDENCE	DRIBBLING	TRICKS	AGILITY	WEAK FOOT
83	88	92	79	85

28

JAMAL MUSIALA

Club: Bayern Munich
Country: Germany
DOB: 26/02/2003

In cricket, commentators talk about "all-rounders" – players who can bowl as well as they can bat! Well, Musiala's an "all-round skiller" – the agile midfielder can dribble just as well with either foot and can produce an outrageous piece of skill to get him out of trouble if needed!

CONFIDENCE	DRIBBLING	TRICKS	AGILITY	WEAK FOOT
85	88	84	91	85

27

LEROY SANE

Club: Bayern Munich
Country: Germany
DOB: 11/01/1996

Bayern Munich's official TikTok account published a video of "Sane's signature move" at the start of 2023 – and, you guessed it, it was the fake shot! When he gets anywhere near the goal, he pretends to pull the trigger with his strong foot, before pushing the ball away in the opposite direction!

CONFIDENCE	DRIBBLING	TRICKS	AGILITY	WEAK FOOT
92	88	89	87	71

TOP SKILL!
THE FAKE SHOT

26
SAID BENRAHMA

Club: West Ham
Country: Algeria
DOB: 10/08/1995

There's only so much showboating you can do when your team is embroiled in a relegation battle, so Benrahma must be bursting to let it all out in 2024! We're hoping he lets loose again and we start seeing the Rainbow Flicks and Sombreros that we got used to during his spell in the Championship with Brentford!

CONFIDENCE	DRIBBLING	TRICKS	AGILITY	WEAK FOOT
85	84	90	85	84

25
BERNARDO SILVA

Club: Man. City
Country: Portugal
DOB: 10/08/1994

If the City squad ever have to pick teams in training, you just know that Bernardo is getting chosen first every single time! His close control and tenacity means he must be up there with the best five-a-side players on the planet – or the worst if you ever have the bad luck to have to play against him!

CONFIDENCE	DRIBBLING	TRICKS	AGILITY	WEAK FOOT
90	92	85	94	72

24
CHRISTOPHER NKUNKU

Club: Chelsea
Country: France
DOB: 14/11/1997

You would think that by suffering some knock backs during 2022-23, Nkunku's rating would also be, well, knocked back! On the contrary, he actually continues his steady rise up the MATCH skills charts, because every time we see him play we're impressed by his top trickery!

CONFIDENCE	DRIBBLING	TRICKS	AGILITY	WEAK FOOT
85	89	90	89	79

23

LUIS DIAZ

Club: Liverpool
Country: Colombia
DOB: 13/01/1997

What do the likes of Wilfried Zaha, Paul Pogba, Yannick Bolasie, Juan Cuadrado and Luis Diaz all have in common? No, it's not that they're all epic ballers (although that's also a fair point)... It's that they all go for the short sleeves and gloves look in winter! Maybe it is an epic baller tradition after all?

CONFIDENCE	DRIBBLING	TRICKS	AGILITY	WEAK FOOT
87	87	88	86	85

22

KINGSLEY COMAN

Club: Bayern Munich
Country: France
DOB: 13/06/1996

We'd love to be a fly on the wall when Coman takes a copy of the 2024 MATCH Football Skills Annual into the Bayern dressing room, because he's overtaken Sane as the club's highest-rated skiller! He'll have to buy one for every team-mate just to rub it in!

CONFIDENCE	DRIBBLING	TRICKS	AGILITY	WEAK FOOT
86	89	91	92	75

21

RODRYGO

TOP SKILL!
LA CROQUETA

Club: Real Madrid
Country: Brazil
DOB: 09/01/2001

Having to defend against Rodrygo is like looking at a really strong optical illusion! He makes you think the ball isn't moving and you've got a chance of nicking it off him, but then suddenly it starts spinning away and you're left in a state of confusion and wondering whether Earth is round after all...

CONFIDENCE	DRIBBLING	TRICKS	AGILITY	WEAK FOOT
87	85	93	88	80

20
MARTIN ODEGAARD

Club: *Arsenal*

Country: *Norway*

DOB: *17/12/1998*

We don't want to distract you from making your way through this year's countdown, but we do need you to take a short break to look up Odegaard's skill against Alex Iwobi in 2022-23! As both players go sliding in for a free ball, the Norway technician pulls out a Rabona while on the floor to leave Iwobi for dead. That was pure filth, Martin!

CONFIDENCE
91

DRIBBLING
88

TRICKS
94

AGILITY
88

WEAK FOOT
72

DIANI

FACTFILE!

DOB: 01/04/1995
Position: Forward
Club: Lyon
Country: France
Boot brand: adidas

DID YOU KNOW?

In the 2022-23 season, with former club PSG, Diani finished as the French league's top scorer for the first time in her career!

FACTFILE!

DOB: *02/09/1999*
Position: *Att. midfielder*
Club: *Man. United*
Country: *England*
Boot brand: *Nike*

DID YOU KNOW?

The Red Devils star played nine matches for rivals Man. City before joining Man. United!

TOONE

BRAIN-BUSTER!

How well do you know some of footy's best tricksters?

1. Name the striker that Khvicha Kvaratskhelia set up more times than any other player in 2022-23?

2. Which German giants did Arsenal sign Vivianne Miedema from back in 2017 – Bayern Munich or Wolfsburg?

3. Did mega tricky winger Kaoru Mitoma bust net at the 2022 World Cup for Japan – yes or no?

4. Which side has Martin Odegaard never played for – Real Betis, Real Sociedad or Real Madrid?

5. The Lionesses' Euro 2022 heroine Chloe Kelly started her career at which London club?

6. Which boot brand has Eberechi Eze had a deal with since 2021 – adidas, Nike or New Balance?

7. True or False? USA superstar Rose Lavelle's middle name is actually "Petal"!

8. Who was Spain superstar Pedri's football idol growing up – Andres Iniesta or Xabi Alonso?

9. How much did Real Madrid pay to sign wonderkid Endrick – more or less than £90 million?

10. True or False? Lyon baller Amel Majri has spent her entire career at the French club!

1 ....
2 ....
3 ....
4 ....
5 ....
6 ....
7 ....
8 ....
9 ....
10 ....

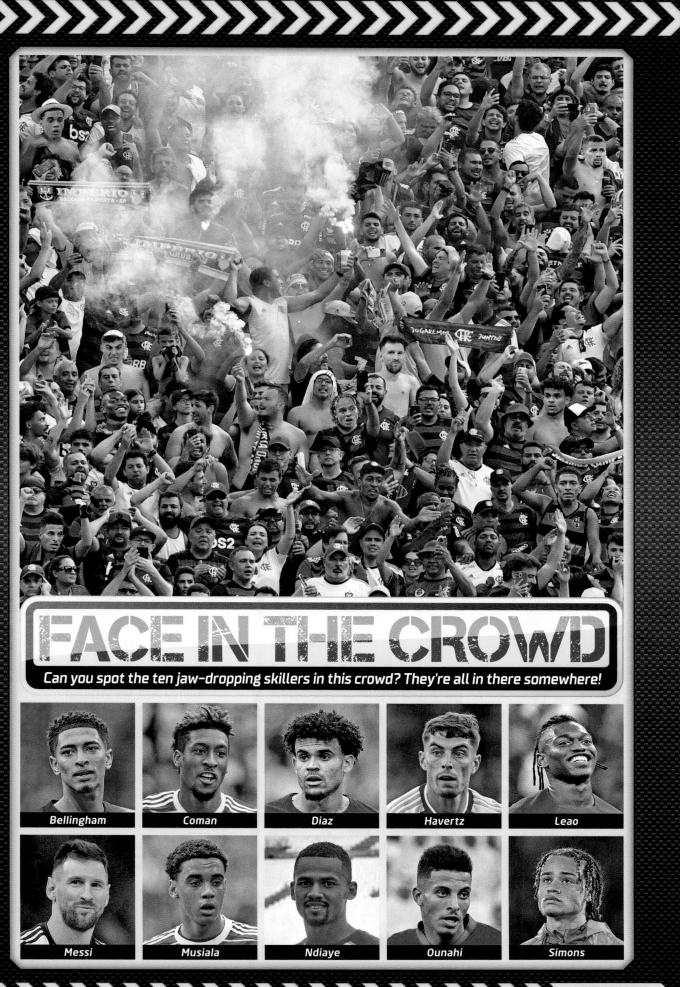

FACE IN THE CROWD

Can you spot the ten jaw-dropping skillers in this crowd? They're all in there somewhere!

Bellingham	Coman	Diaz	Havertz	Leao
Messi	Musiala	Ndiaye	Ounahi	Simons

ANSWERS ON PAGE 60

19

MOHAMED SALAH

Club: *Liverpool*
Country: *Egypt*
DOB: *15/06/1992*

One of Liverpool fans' favourite moments of the entire 2022-23 campaign was seeing Salah sit Man. United defender Lisandro Martinez on his bottom at Anfield! All it took were a couple of simple ball roll cuts, before he passed the ball into Cody Gakpo's path to finish past David de Gea!

CONFIDENCE
93

DRIBBLING
90

TRICKS
88

AGILITY
90

WEAK FOOT
73

18

RAPHINHA

Club: *Barcelona*
Country: *Brazil*
DOB: *14/12/1996*

Not everyone can cope with the demands of playing for Barcelona, with their fans super spoilt from having the likes of Ronaldinho, Lionel Messi and Neymar in attack over the years! Raphinha's confidence took a hit in 2022-23 but we know he can still deliver the goods!

TOP SKILL!
THE SCISSOR

CONFIDENCE	DRIBBLING	TRICKS	AGILITY	WEAK FOOT
86	88	90	88	84

17

MARCUS RASHFORD

Club: *Man. United*
Country: *England*
DOB: *31/10/1997*

We're pretty sure Rashford got a copy of last year's Skills Annual and saw himself down in 38th place, because since it was released he's been on absolute flames! Everything he touched turned to gold at the start of 2023 and The Red Devils have definitely overrelied on him this year!

CONFIDENCE	DRIBBLING	TRICKS	AGILITY	WEAK FOOT
93	88	91	85	80

16

JOAO FELIX

Club: *Barcelona*
Country: *Portugal*
DOB: *10/11/1999*

It feels like Felix has been around for ages but he was only 23 at the start of the 2023-24 campaign! He made his Benfica debut at the age of 17 and has already played in two of Europe's top five leagues. We wouldn't put it past him to complete the set before he retires!

CONFIDENCE	DRIBBLING	TRICKS	AGILITY	WEAK FOOT
88	86	89	88	87

15

LIONEL MESSI

TOP SKILL!
THE BODY SWERVE

Club: Inter Miami
Country: Argentina
DOB: 24/06/1987

Winning the 2022 World Cup and Golden Ball award was the cherry on top of a legendary career for a player who many consider to be the GOAT! His sky-high confidence and laser vision mean he can still be the best player on the pitch at 36 years old – plus he topped the Ligue 1 dribbling charts last season!

CONFIDENCE 99	DRIBBLING 89	TRICKS 80	AGILITY 87	WEAK FOOT 83

14

KAORU MITOMA

Club: Brighton
Country: Japan
DOB: 20/05/1997

There's nobody more qualified on this year's countdown than the Seagulls star! Mitoma completed a physical education degree and did his final essay on the art of dribbling, which involved him wearing a GoPro during games to work out how best to take on his man. Okay, brainiac!

CONFIDENCE 90	DRIBBLING 91	TRICKS 87	AGILITY 91	WEAK FOOT 79

13

GABRIEL MARTINELLI

Club: Arsenal
Country: Brazil
DOB: 18/06/2001

There are players in the Prem, like Kevin De Bruyne and Bruno Fernandes, that scare defenders when their heads are raised because they know that they're spotting their next killer ball. With Martinelli, it's the exact opposite – once he gets his head down and starts running there's no stopping him!

CONFIDENCE 90	DRIBBLING 88	TRICKS 90	AGILITY 92	WEAK FOOT 78

12
RAFAEL LEAO

Club: AC Milan
Country: Portugal
DOB: 10/06/1999

Nobody dribbles quite like Leao! Not even you when you were a baby and you had an "airplane" of food flying towards you! He completed more dribbles than any other player in Serie A in 2022-23 and was just behind Vinicius Jr. in the take-on charts in the Champions League!

CONFIDENCE	DRIBBLING	TRICKS	AGILITY	WEAK FOOT
89	92	89	84	86

11
ANTONY

Club: Man. United
Country: Brazil
DOB: 24/02/2000

Haters will say that Man. United overspent on the Brazil winger and he "flopped" in 2022-23. Antony will say, "shhhh"! Even if the former Ajax star sometimes frustrates Red Devils fans with his lack of end product, there's no denying his showboat status – his 360-degree spin is basically copyrighted!

CONFIDENCE	DRIBBLING	TRICKS	AGILITY	WEAK FOOT
93	88	95	96	78

TOP SKILL!
STUTTER FEINT

10
JADON SANCHO

Club: Man. United
Country: England
DOB: 25/03/2000

Injuries definitely took their toll on JS during the 2022-23 season, and he still hasn't reached fifth gear in a Man. United shirt! Thankfully for Red Devils fans, they're gonna know when he does – his skills are louder than a 7-litre sports car engine travelling at full throttle!

CONFIDENCE	DRIBBLING	TRICKS	AGILITY	WEAK FOOT
85	92	95	91	82

SKILLS ICON NO.3
MARADONA

Maradona received his first football as a present when he was just three years old and soon became obsessed with the game. He made his senior debut in Argentina when he was 15 and quickly attracted attention from Europe's biggest clubs. After a two-season spell with Barcelona, he moved to Napoli and became a legend, winning two Serie A titles there. His greatest moment came at the 1986 World Cup, however, where he captained his nation to the trophy and scored one of the tournament's best-ever individual goals against England. We just won't mention the Hand of God...

FACTPACK!

Full name: *Diego Armando Maradona*

DOB: *30/10/1960*

Height: *5ft 5in*

Country: *Argentina*

Caps: *91*

Goals: *34*

CAREER LEAGUE STATS

Date	Club	Games	Goals
1976-1981	Argentinos Juniors	166	116
1981-1982	Boca Juniors	40	28
1982-1984	Barcelona	36	22
1984-1991	Napoli	188	81
1992-1993	Sevilla	26	5
1993-1994	Newell's Old Boys	5	0
1995-1997	Boca Juniors	30	7

DID YOU KNOW?

HE PLAYED ONE GAME IN A TOTTENHAM SHIRT – IT WAS A TESTIMONIAL FOR THEIR FORMER ARGENTINE PLAYER OSSIE ARDILES!

TOP SKILL!
THE MARADONA TURN

CONFIDENCE
100

DRIBBLING
99

TRICKS
100

AGILITY
93

WEAK FOOT
75

SHOWREEL!

Scan the QR code to watch some of his best bits!

MAGULL

FACTFILE!

DOB: *15/08/1994*
Position: *Midfielder*
Club: *Bayern Munich*
Country: *Germany*
Boot brand: *adidas*

DID YOU KNOW?

She earned the nickname "Little Magician" because of her ability to pull off skills!

MARTENS

FACTFILE!

DOB: 16/12/1992
Position: Winger
Club: PSG
Country: Netherlands
Boot brand: Nike

DID YOU KNOW?

She's been compared in the past to all-time Netherlands legend Johan Cruyff!

9

KHVICHA KVARATSKHELIA

Club: Napoli

Country: Georgia

DOB: 12/02/2001

We've sent a top-secret report to the FBI on the Georgia talent because we're pretty sure he's a UFO from another planet! Some of the runs he goes on are out of this world, and there's no surprise that the Napoli supporters refer to him as "Kvaradona" after legendary former player Diego Maradona!

CONFIDENCE
90

DRIBBLING
92

TRICKS
86

AGILITY
91

WEAK FOOT
89

8

MYKHAYLO MUDRYK

Club: *Chelsea*
Country: *Ukraine*
DOB: 05/01/2001

MATCH was repping Mudryk before it was fashionable! Look back at last year's Skills Annual and you'll find him in 42nd spot, with a disclaimer saying that once he signed for a big European club he'd shoot up the rankings. Premier League scouts were clearly paying attention to us then!

CONFIDENCE	DRIBBLING	TRICKS	AGILITY	WEAK FOOT
85	90	95	90	88

7

WILFRIED ZAHA

Club: *Galatasaray*
Country: *Ivory Coast*
DOB: 10/11/1992

Stick both hands up if you've ever been on a really long trip and got bored out of your mind! Instead of asking "how long's left?" for the 100th time, MATCH recommends sticking on a Zaha skills compilation on YouTube and letting time fly by. Oh, and pick up this Annual from the floor if you dropped it when you put both hands up!

CONFIDENCE	DRIBBLING	TRICKS	AGILITY	WEAK FOOT
95	88	95	89	81

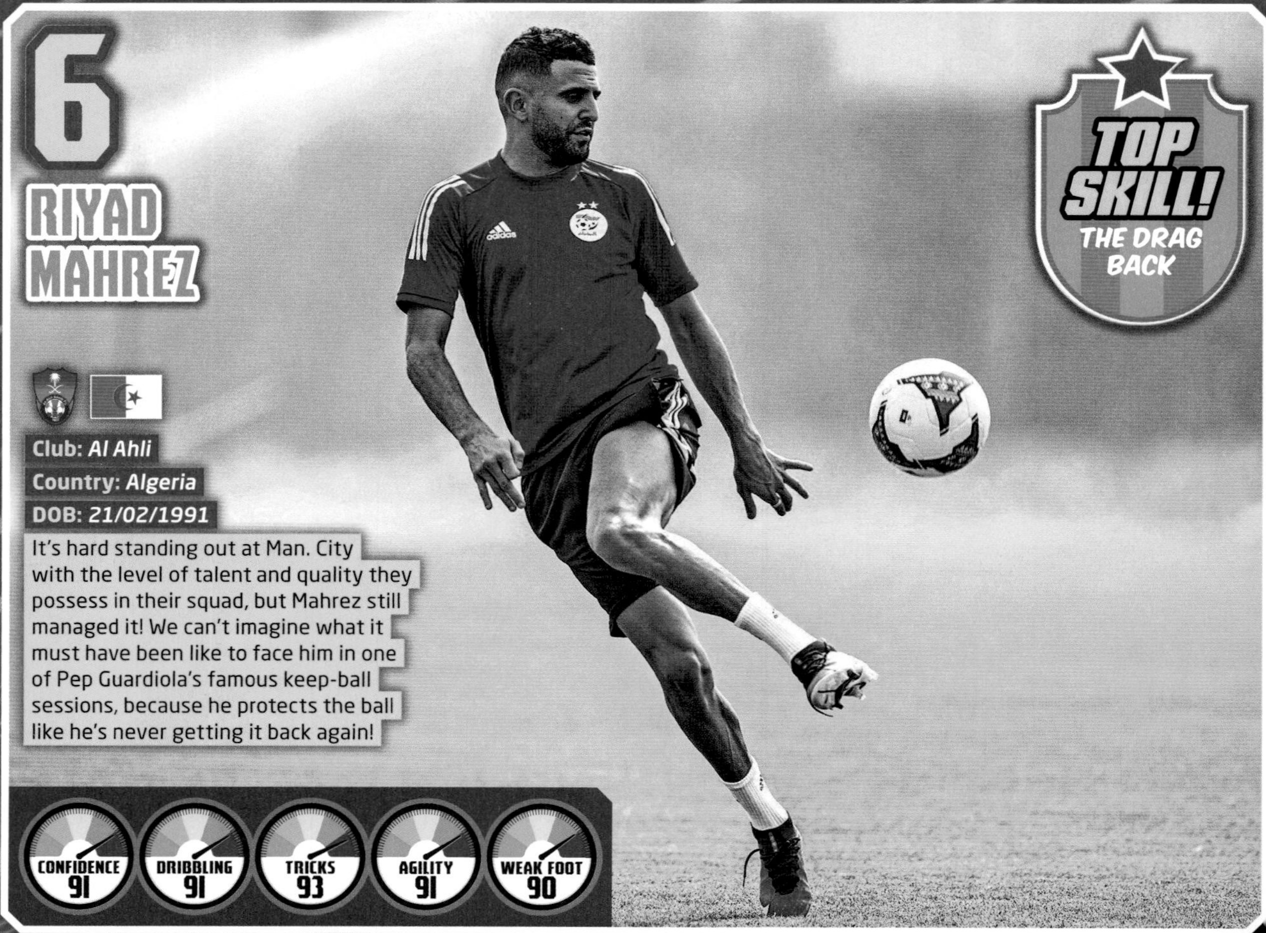

6

RIYAD MAHREZ

TOP SKILL! THE DRAG BACK

Club: *Al Ahli*
Country: *Algeria*
DOB: *21/02/1991*

It's hard standing out at Man. City with the level of talent and quality they possess in their squad, but Mahrez still managed it! We can't imagine what it must have been like to face him in one of Pep Guardiola's famous keep-ball sessions, because he protects the ball like he's never getting it back again!

CONFIDENCE	DRIBBLING	TRICKS	AGILITY	WEAK FOOT
91	91	93	91	90

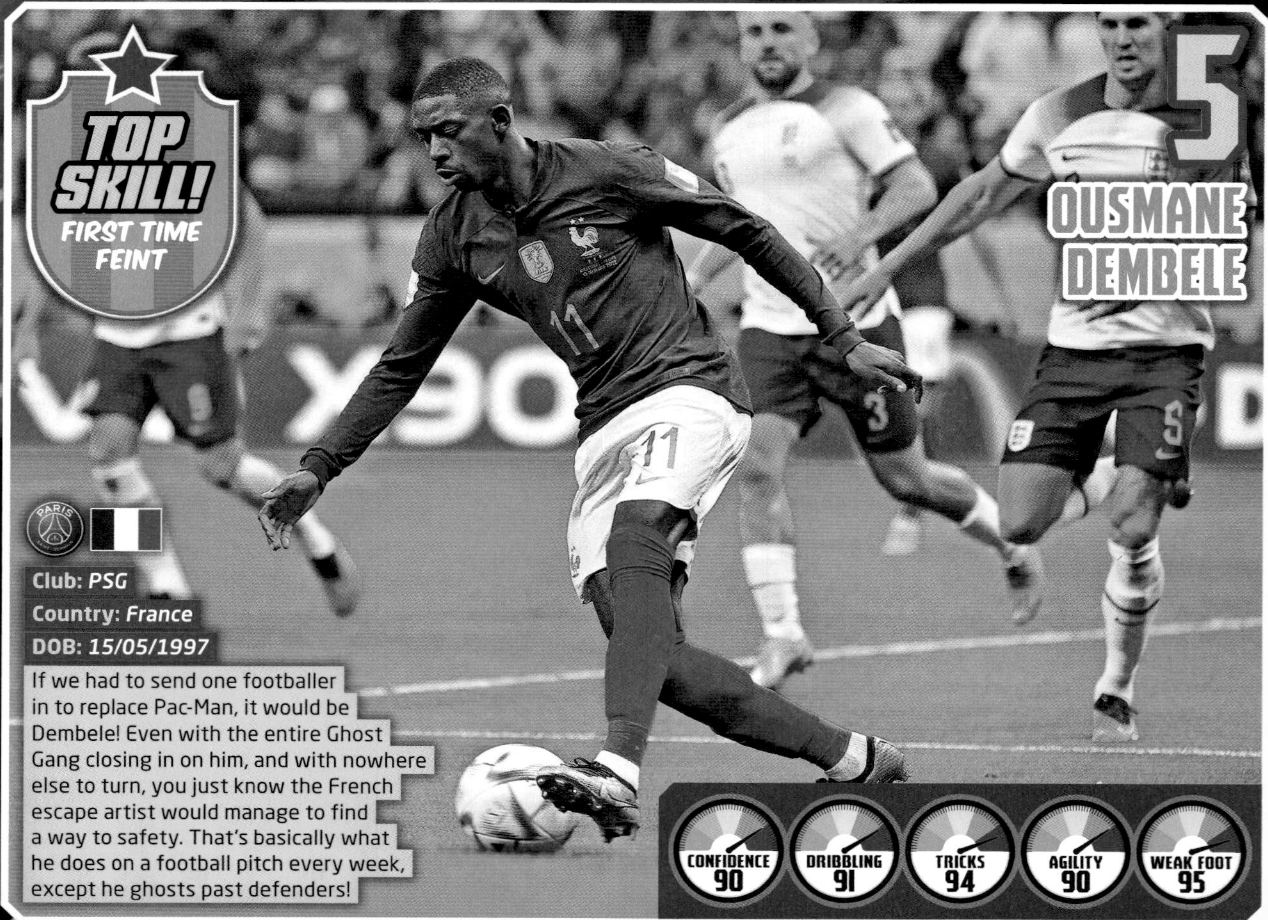

5

OUSMANE DEMBELE

TOP SKILL! FIRST TIME FEINT

Club: *PSG*
Country: *France*
DOB: *15/05/1997*

If we had to send one footballer in to replace Pac-Man, it would be Dembele! Even with the entire Ghost Gang closing in on him, and with nowhere else to turn, you just know the French escape artist would manage to find a way to safety. That's basically what he does on a football pitch every week, except he ghosts past defenders!

CONFIDENCE	DRIBBLING	TRICKS	AGILITY	WEAK FOOT
90	91	94	90	95

4

ALLAN SAINT-MAXIMIN

TOP SKILL!
THE CHOP

DID YOU KNOW?

ONLY ONE OTHER NEWCASTLE PLAYER COMPLETED MORE TAKE-ONS THAN SAINT-MAXIMIN IN 2022-23, DESPITE HIM PLAYING 50% FEWER MINUTES THAN THEIR NEXT-BEST DRIBBLER!

Club: *Al Ahli*
Country: *France*
DOB: *12/03/1997*

CONFIDENCE 93
DRIBBLING 93
TRICKS 95
AGILITY 93
WEAK FOOT 88

By leaving Newcastle in the summer of 2023, Saint-Maximin threw away the opportunity to be named our top-rated Premier League skiller for the second year running! Surely that's way more important than whatever crazy money he's earning in the Saudi Pro League?

CROSSWORD

Use the clues below to fill in MATCH's tricky crossword!

ACROSS

4. A very similar skill to the Sombrero Flick! (7)

5. Italian club Colombia trickster Lady Andrade used to tear it up for! (5)

7. Foot that Algeria ace Riyad Mahrez would say is his strongest! (4)

9. Portuguese legend who won trophies at Porto, Chelsea and Barcelona! (4)

10. Country Alisha Lehmann represents! (11)

12. Joao Felix's football idol from Brazil! (4)

14. In Spanish, a nutmeg is known as a _ _ _ _ _ _! Clue: driving. (6)

17. Mohamed Salah is the Egyptian _ _ _ _! (4)

18. Zlatan Ibrahimovic, AKA... _ _ _ _! (4)

19. Boot brand Man. City superstar Jack Grealish laces up in! (4)

DOWN

1. Month Arsenal wing wizard Gabriel Martinelli was born! (4)

2. WSL club Tobin Heath spent one season at in the 2021-22 season! (7)

3. The city Willian has spent the majority of his career playing in! (6)

6. Premier League club Bukayo Saka had a sweet spot for as a child because of his father! (9)

8. All-time Brazil legend known for his tricks and net-busting skills! (4)

9. Scandinavian country Erin Cuthbert scored her first Scotland goal against back in 2017! (7)

11. Lionel Messi's long-standing nickname! (3,4)

13. World champion women freestyler whose surname is Mnich! (6)

15. MATCH's No.1 skiller in our 2020 Annual! (6)

16. Finish the Skill Move, The Bolasie _ _ _ _ _! (5)

WHO STARTED WHERE?

Have a go at matching these trick machines with the clubs they started their careers at!

WILFRIED GNONTO	SAID BENRAHMA	MICHAEL OLISE	NABIL FEKIR	AMAD DIALLO	MEMPHIS DEPAY
1	2	3	4	5	6

A	B	C	D	E	F
OLYMPIQUE LYONNAIS	READING FOOTBALL CLUB EST. 1871	FCZ	OGC NICE DEPSI 1904	PSV	ATALANTA 1907
LYON	READING	FC ZURICH	NICE	PSV	ATALANTA

ODD ONE OUT!

Allan Saint-Maximin

Jadon Sancho

Roberto Firmino

Bernardo Silva

Thiago Alcantara

Which of these top-quality ballers has NEVER played in Germany's Bundesliga?

Douglas Costa

ANSWER ON PAGE

MATCH!
WOMEN SKILLERS

HARDER

FACTFILE!

DOB: 15/11/1992
Position: Forward
Club: Bayern Munich
Country: Denmark
Boot brand: Nike

DID YOU KNOW?

She joined Chelsea in 2020 for what was then a world-record fee for a female footballer!

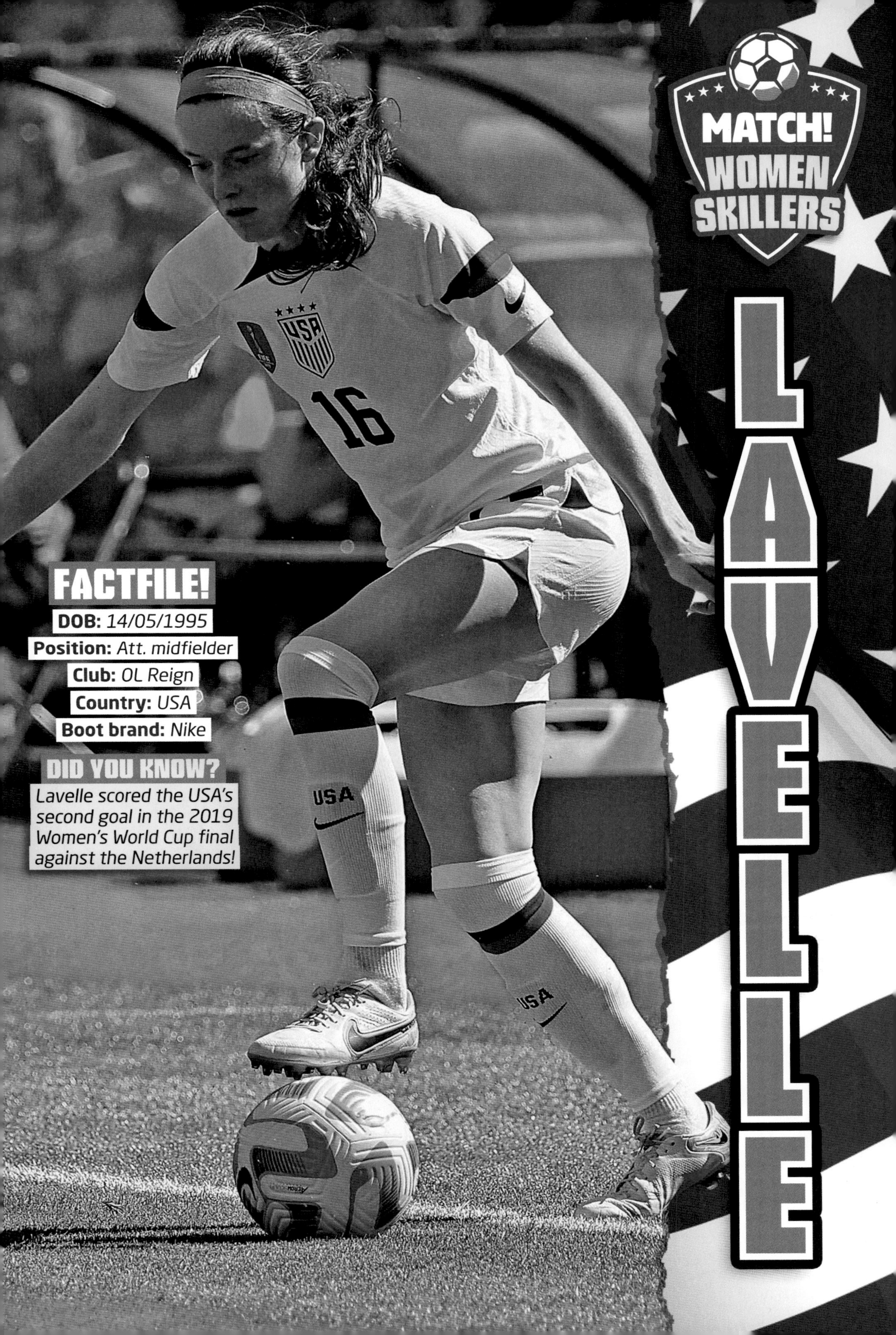

FACTFILE!

DOB: *14/05/1995*
Position: *Att. midfielder*
Club: *OL Reign*
Country: *USA*
Boot brand: *Nike*

DID YOU KNOW?

Lavelle scored the USA's
second goal in the 2019
Women's World Cup final
against the Netherlands!

LAVELLE

3

KYLIAN MBAPPE

TOP SKILL!
THE FAKE RABONA

CONFIDENCE 98

DRIBBLING 94

TRICKS 95

AGILITY 93

WEAK FOOT 88

Club: *PSG*
Country: *France*
DOB: *20/12/1998*

DID YOU KNOW?
IN MARCH 2023, MBAPPE BECAME PSG'S ALL-TIME TOP GOALSCORER AT JUST 24 YEARS OLD!

MATCH reckons the France star should become an inventor once he retires from footy! Not any sort of inventor, though – we don't want him designing new toothbrushes! We need him to come up with some silky skill moves, the sort that would get five-star reviews from the likes of Neymar and Lionel Messi!

2
NEYMAR

DID YOU KNOW?

IN 2023, NEYMAR SCORED HIS 150TH LEAGUE GOAL IN EUOPEAN FOOTY — 68 FOR BARCELONA AND 82 FOR PSG!

TOP SKILL!
THE SOMBRERO FLICK

Club: *Al Hilal*
Country: *Brazil*
DOB: *05/02/1992*

MASSIVE news everyone, Neymar has been dethroned for the first time in five years... We have a new No.1! But before you find out who it is (yeah, alright, we know you've already looked) let's take a moment to appreciate Neymar's reign. If it wasn't for all of his injuries in 2023, he'd probably still be occupying the top spot, so watch this space for next year!

CONFIDENCE
96

DRIBBLING
95

TRICKS
98

AGILITY
92

WEAK FOOT
89

TURN THE PAGE TO FIND OUT WHO'S OUR NO.1!

MATCH! 49

1

VINICIUS JR.

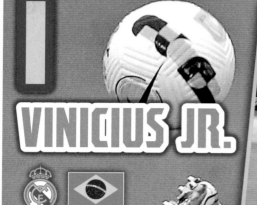

Club: *Real Madrid*
Country: *Brazil*
DOB: *12/07/2000*

Football Skills fans, bow down to your new king: King Vini! Or maybe that should be King Vini I as it's his first time on the throne! Either way, the Los Blancos baller deserves the limelight, as he's been irresistibly good over the last year, humiliating defenders with his Samba sorcery and devilishly direct dribbling!

TOP SKILL!
SCOOP TURN FAKE

DID YOU KNOW?
VINICIUS WAS DIRECTLY INVOLVED IN 30 GOALS FROM HIS FIRST 45 CHAMPIONS LEAGUE APPEARANCES!

CONFIDENCE 97

DRIBBLING 95

TRICKS 96

AGILITY 96

WEAK FOOT 88

STAT ATTACK!

VINICIUS JR.

We check out some of the sickest stats and facts from the new king of skills!

5,400+

Across the big five European leagues since 2021-22, Vini leads all attacking players for total carry distance - over 5,400 metres. Wow!

45+

Since the start of 2021-22, Vini has more than 45 league goals and assists combined!

47

The Real Madrid superstar completed more dribbles than any other Champions League player in 2022-23!

100

He became the youngest foreign player in history to play 100 matches for Real Madrid!

10+

He bagged at least ten goals and assists combined in the past two Champo League campaigns as well!

22

The trickster is the youngest visiting player to score twice v Liverpool at Anfield in major European competition since Johan Cruyff in December 1966!

112

No one completed more successful dribbles in La Liga last term than Vini!

64

No Los Blancos baller created more chances for their team-mates than Vini in 2022-23!

122

No one was fouled more times than Vinicius in La Liga in 2022-23!

2

Vinicius is the second youngest player to score in three consecutive games for Real Madrid in the Champions League!

1

He scored the first World Cup goal of his career in the win over South Korea in December 2022!

PICK YOUR TOP 5 FAVE SKILLERS!

RODRYGO
Real Madrid & Brazil

JESUS
Arsenal & Brazil

FODEN
Man. City & England

For the chance to win a Nacon RIG 300 PRO gaming headset, just write down your five favourite tricksters, fill out your contact details and email a photograph of this page to: **match.magazine@kelsey.co.uk**
Closing date: January 21, 2024. One lucky winner will be picked at random.

1.

2.

3.

4.

5.

NAME:

DATE OF BIRTH:

ADDRESS:

MOBILE:

EMAIL:

ZIDANE

Zizou wasn't a typical showman in the sense that he didn't just do tricks for the sake of it, but he oozed flair with every touch and had the technique of a king. His volleyed goal in the final of the 2002 Champions League is widely regarded as one of the tournament's best-ever finishes. He also had plenty of success with France, who he helped to win the 1998 World Cup with two goals in the final, before being named Player of the Tournament at the 2000 European Championship as Les Bleus picked up back-to-back victories!

FACTPACK!

Full name: *Zinedine Yazid Zidane*

DOB: *23/06/1972*

Height: *6ft 1in*

Country: *France*

Caps: *108*

Goals: *31*

CAREER LEAGUE STATS

Date	Club	Games	Goals
1989-1992	Cannes	61	6
1992-1996	Bordeaux	139	28
1996-2001	Juventus	151	24
2001-2006	Real Madrid	155	37

TOP SKILL!
THE ROULETTE

DID YOU KNOW?

HIS TRANSFER TO REAL MADRID IN 2001 FROM JUVENTUS WAS A WORLD RECORD FEE AT THE TIME OF €77.5 MILLION!

CONFIDENCE
99

DRIBBLING
97

TRICKS
98

AGILITY
80

WEAK FOOT
97

SHOWREEL!

Scan the QR code to watch some of his best bits!

WORDSEARCH

Can you find 30 skill-themed words in the giant grid below?

```
X E B L
H W O Q
Q G X J
E C U R
F M K C
```

```
H N B C
J M G M
Y I D H
Q J P T
J K I T
```

```
N J C Q I H A B I L Y N N P N N X U X W I C S K W I L H I E
Q K M O N G B G A B P F C V T A J S R E K K E T O B B B C C
Y I T A O J F L K Y G Y C N T N S X U E B N F Y B H E R K H
G B M B R B M M U M N M W F I C U I K K X Y R I N D A I S N
S R Y G G N D B K I S X G H O S U E T S S V E A I U I D V I
K G E X C X D O T F G Q X D R L B C U Z B Y E P A X J G X O
C B I E H F U I M R F D E Q P T Y F R C A A S D R L B E R U
R Y D C M X I Q U D S B C D X O F O N O L Q T E E X Z V R E
U B L Z V H J U I R A M U V V L M F S L L K Y R K O O U V U
Y Q R Y W Y M M U D A Q A P S U R N X L E C L I I J T T D B
Q A O I Z B K F E W N S S V X M R U I Y R O E S N N L F K B
J Y W A H O L G B U G K O N O L Q T N S N K M N U L Z V S L
P B A B T H O N M Z F I M C M T G N N W V C Z N E X Y H K J
X W M D X C I X D F N L K Q X E O E N F D I L Z B Z C F Q O
M G X O Z T S A F G A L J W J H C G I S T L E J T L W H B A
R P C U S A D Z S V F N F K W W S N I G L F I Q Z Y X P H Q
E O M O C L A S I N U W C L P A O T V Z T C S N R J B B H H
V H U Z O E E E Y Z B S I Y R T M O T Z C F Q O Z E F T I D
O D T C O N F P E V C Z N G D U B T H R M O S R R W I H J A
P U B C P T O N Z J I R L W Q W R N M X I I I T E V Z V C I
E H P Q T T O P L J P A O A J J E W L W G C T F S T O D G O
T O U J K V A R M K V F O U F H R J A O U O K D U O V W J D
S C M T A N U P J F R U L R L B O D H K Z C H S E Z Q Z Y R
D N E J N F V R T O E E E O K Q E O S D F A V N L T X C A W I
X U Q A D U P S E P G S W H M S T Q Q K O J T Q H E H F L L
N S G W W X J L U P F U H F A V M T L Z B N N G F F R J I L
H F E N F R B F C L S E J O X M T P E V I J A W E X H I I S
N N B B J B C Z A P D C S C X S Q Q H E L W C M N F N P Z X
B J I V I T V I R Q X A P I I R J C F T A O B W O H S K V S
D V N R M F R K N A G P D T U N J Y G K J X E Q E N P K M S
V W D F H I F X E L U M Z S J F I D M V T M A G I C L U B I
P W J U R X O N F K S A F A E J F R S N I C O N T R O L N P
S B X K R B T P C I P A Q L J Z S I B U X E D A F G W F C Q
C R H K F I Z I N S E S S E A X M I D E W P S E S S Q C O D
S X M I R R K H Y F M R U T R T O S T W L F C L C L Y R R O
```

Baller	Elastico	Kickup	Sauce	Talent
Bridge	Fancy	Magic	Scoop	Technique
Control	Feint	Nutmeg	Showboat	Tekkers
Dribble	Flair	Panna	Skill	Trickster
Drills	Flick	Rainbow	Sombrero	Turn
Dummy	Freestyle	Roulette	Stepover	Worldie

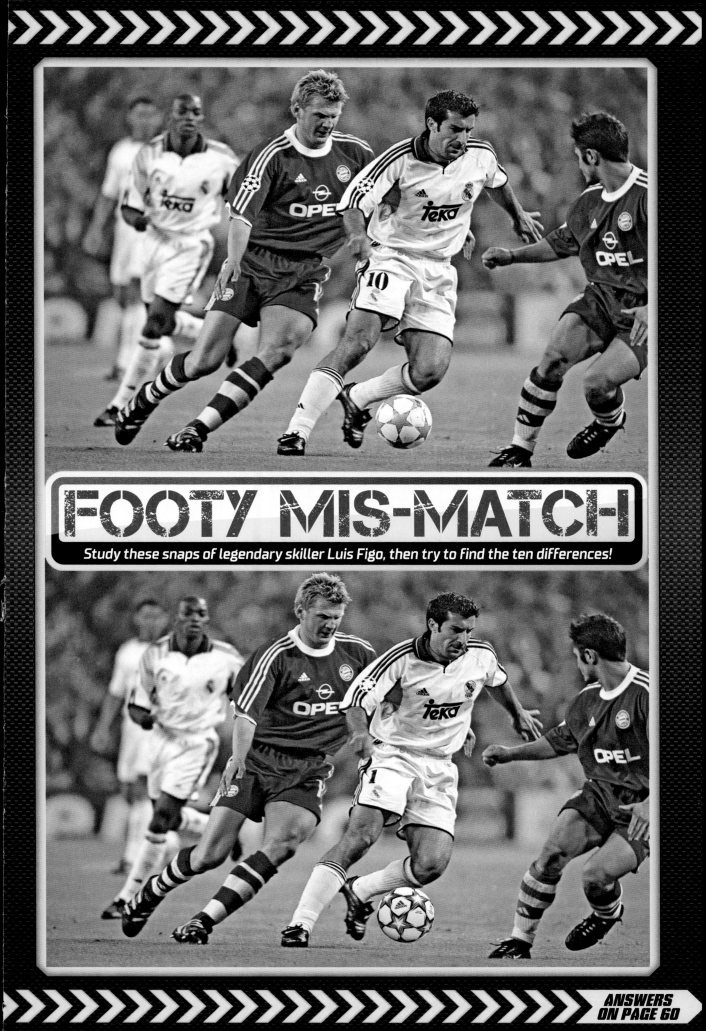

FOOTY MIS-MATCH

Study these snaps of legendary skiller Luis Figo, then try to find the ten differences!

ANSWERS ON PAGE 60

Wordfit P20

Debinha Quiz P21

1. 32 years old;
2. No.99;
3. North Carolina Courage;
4. More than 125 caps;
5. False.

Spot The Ball P21

I7.

Brain-Buster P30

1. Victor Osimhen;
2. Bayern Munich;
3. No;
4. Real Betis;
5. Arsenal;
6. New Balance;
7. False;
8. Andres Iniesta;
9. Less than £90 million;
10. True.

Who Started Where? P45

1C;
2D;
3B;
4A;
5F;
6E.

Odd One Out P45

Bernardo Silva.

Face In The Crowd P31

Crossword P44

Wordsearch P58

WORDSEARCH
Find 30 jaw-dropping skill moves in the giant grid below!

Footy Mis-Match P59

LOVE MATCH?
GET IT DELIVERED EVERY FORTNIGHT!

GIFT!

PANINI **2023 PREMIER LEAGUE OFFICIAL STICKERS!**

PACKED EVERY ISSUE WITH...

- ★ Red-hot gear
- ★ News & gossip
- ★ Stats & quizzes
- ★ Massive stars
- ★ Posters & pics
- & loads more!

ONLY £3 PER ISSUE!
£39 FOR 13 ISSUES*

HOW TO SUBSCRIBE TO MATCH!

CALL 📱
01959 543 747
QUOTE: MATAN24

ONLINE 📱
SHOP.KELSEY.CO.UK/
MATAN24